BULLYING

BULLYING

BY LAURA PERDEW

CONTENT CONSULTANT
SALLY KUYKENDALL
CHAIR AND ASSOCIATE PROFESSOR
SAINT JOSEPH'S UNIVERSITY

Essential Library

An Imprint of Abdo Publishing | www.abdopublishing.com

www.abdopublishing.com

Published by Abdo Publishing, a division of ABDO, PO Box 398166, Minneapolis, Minnesota 55439. Copyright © 2015 by Abdo Consulting Group, Inc. International copyrights reserved in all countries. No part of this book may be reproduced in any form without written permission from the publisher. Essential Library™ is a trademark and logo of Abdo Publishing.

Printed in the United States of America, North Mankato, Minnesota
032014
092014

THIS BOOK CONTAINS
RECYCLED MATERIALS

Cover Photo: Fuse/Thinkstock
Interior Photos: Fuse/Thinkstock, 2, 42, 46; iStockphoto, 6, 36, 56; Michael S. Gordon/AP Images, 10; Jacob Wackerhausen/Thinkstock, 14; Shutterstock Images, 16, 90; Thinkstock, 22, 60, 69; Mubadda Rohana/Thinkstock, 24; Jupiter Images/Thinkstock, 26; Kim Berrywood/Thinkstock, 31; O Driscoll Imaging/Shutterstock Images, 34; Vitchanan Photography/Shutterstock Images, 39; Leah Marshall/Thinkstock, 51; Monkey Business Images/Shutterstock Images, 54; Wavebreakmedia/Thinkstock, 63; Digital Vision/Thinkstock, 65; Anne-Louise Quarfoth/Thinkstock, 66; Rogelio Solis/AP Images, 72; The Ledger, Calvin Knight/AP Images, 76; Ashland Daily Press/AP Images, 79; Ron Edmonds/AP Images, 82; The Ledger, Rick Runion/AP Images, 86; Jakov Cordina/Thinkstock, 93

Editor: Jenna Gleisner
Series Designer: Becky Daum

Library of Congress Control Number: 2014932560

Cataloging-in-Publication Data

Perdew, Laura.
 Bullying / Laura Perdew.
  p. cm. -- (Essential issues)
Includes bibliographical references and index.
ISBN 978-1-62403-418-3
1. Bullying--Juvenile literature. 2. Aggressiveness in children--Juvenile literature. I. Title.
302.34--dc23

2014932560

CONTENTS

CHAPTER 1

THE NEW GIRL   6

CHAPTER 2

WHAT IS BULLYING?   16

CHAPTER 3

CYBERBULLYING   26

CHAPTER 4

THE BULLY   36

CHAPTER 5

THE BULLIED   46

CHAPTER 6

THE BYSTANDER   56

CHAPTER 7

THE EFFECTS OF BULLYING   66

CHAPTER 8

LEGISLATION   76

CHAPTER 9

TAKING ACTION   86

Timeline   96
Essential Facts   100
Glossary   102
Additional Resources   104
Source Notes   106
Index   110
About the Author   112
About the Consultant   112

CHAPTER
ONE

THE NEW GIRL

In the fall of 2009, Phoebe Prince moved from Ireland to the United States with her mother and younger sister. Their new home was in the small town of South Hadley, Massachusetts, where Phoebe began her freshman year at South Hadley High School. By all accounts, Phoebe was sociable and well liked, and she performed well academically. In November, she started seeing Sean Mulveyhill, a senior football player. The relationship lasted only a few weeks and ended shortly after Thanksgiving. Nonetheless, the relationship generated insults from some of the other girls at school, including Sean's ex-girlfriend, whom the *Boston Globe* later dubbed "mean girls."[1] The fire was further fueled when Phoebe briefly dated senior Austin Renaud and remained friends with him following the short-lived relationship.

According to other students at the high school, the group of "mean girls" began taunting and harassing Phoebe. They followed her around, calling her names.

Teens who are less popular or new to a community may be targets for bullying.

They verbally assaulted her in the hallways and even in the library. They also regularly knocked books out of Phoebe's hands and threw objects at her. And the girls hung pictures of Phoebe with her face scribbled out on the school walls.

Worse still, for Phoebe, was that there was no escape from the bullying. Even when she was not in school, the girls bullied her in cyberspace. The bullying escalated to harassment. Phoebe was harassed through social media and threatened via text messages.

As Phoebe suffered, school staff members were aware of the relentless harassment. Phoebe's mother had even spoken directly with at least two school personnel about the bullying. Yet the school staff remained silent. No one acted on reports of harassment. No one stepped in to help Phoebe.

The harassment became intolerable. On January 14, 2010, Phoebe was harassed and menaced once again at school. After school, as Phoebe walked home, a car drove by and a girl threw a soda can at Phoebe. The girl also suggested Phoebe should kill herself. Phoebe could not take it anymore. Her younger sister found her that afternoon, hanging in the stairwell of their family home.

Even after Phoebe's death, the cruelty did not end. On the memorial Facebook page set up for Phoebe, some of the "mean girls" posted malicious comments. Moreover, the girls who had relentlessly tormented Phoebe when she was alive continued mocking her when they returned to school.

An Investigation Leads to Charges

The investigation into what led to Phoebe's death took time, and people in Phoebe's community were frustrated the bullies had not faced any punishment. Some even

WHO IS TO BLAME?

After months of being bullied, Phoebe Prince committed suicide. Following her death, a heated debate began over the degree to which the bullies were actually responsible for Phoebe's suicide. The fact that Phoebe was psychologically vulnerable made assessing blame that much more difficult. In Phoebe's case, there was a history of self-injury, hospitalization, and depression, as well as troubles with girls at previous schools. Further, students at South Hadley recalled Phoebe had conflicts with different groups of peers, not simply the pack of "mean girls." Also, far from being a victim, Phoebe was frequently the one with the power because she was popular with the boys and allegedly pulled them away from other relationships. Ultimately, the actions of Phoebe's peers are shameful and unforgivable. But whether they were responsible for her death is a question revealing how ill-equipped the law is to deal with such cases.

Ashley Longe, *left*, and Flannery Mullins, *right*, were two of the six teens charged with felonies for bullying Phoebe Prince.

believed the students connected to Phoebe's bullying should not have been allowed to return to school. One high school parent worried the school's inaction condoned the bullying behavior and sent the wrong message to the student body.

Finally, in March 2010, charges were filed against six teens from South Hadley High School in connection with Phoebe's case. The teens were charged with multiple felonies, the most serious types of crime in the US legal system. Felonies also carry the most severe punishments. The felony charges, including harassment and stalking, were abnormally harsh for a bullying case. District Attorney Elizabeth Scheibel said, "The investigation revealed relentless activities

DIGNITY FOR EVERY STUDENT

Prior to Phoebe's death, the Massachusetts state legislature was working on antibullying laws. Phoebe's death gave the bill momentum, as did the death of 11-year-old Carl Joseph Walker-Hoover, who killed himself after repeatedly being called gay. In May 2010, legislators unanimously passed the Dignity for Every Student bill. It focuses on bullying prevention and education. Antibullying curriculum is now mandatory in all grades in both private and public schools across Massachusetts. In addition, all adults associated with schools, from bus drivers to principals, are required to attend training to identify and act on bullying. Adults are also now legally required to report bullying. The goal in Massachusetts is to change school culture to one in which bullying is not tolerated by students or teachers and bystanders are empowered to act.

directed toward Phoebe to make it impossible for her to stay at school," and that the bullies' conduct "far exceeded the limits of normal teenage relationship-related quarrels."[2]

Also part of the investigation was the negligence of school staff by not helping Phoebe even though they knew of the bullying. Scheibel called this lack of action "troublesome" yet could not find any laws broken.[3] Some questioned whether the students being prosecuted had even broken any laws. The district attorney's office was criticized for overcharging the teens in what some saw as normal behavior. However, the office stood by the case, saying the charges were justifiable based on available evidence.

Five teens charged in Phoebe's case, including Sean,

IS BULLYING A CRIME?

When a person who has been bullied commits suicide, law enforcement is left to determine when cruel, bullying behavior actually becomes criminal. Once upon a time, bullying was simply considered part of growing up—a rite of passage. Now, bullying is a high-stakes topic in schools, communities, and law enforcement as people grapple with antibullying policies. Each state deals with bullying law and policy differently. Some states include criminal sanctions for bullies in their laws, while other states do not have any penalties for bullying. For the most part, schools address bullying issues, and most states require antibullying policies at the school level. Still, if bullying becomes criminal, law enforcement must step in.

ultimately pleaded guilty to lesser charges of criminal harassment in May 2011. Three of the teens received probation and 100 hours each of community service, while the other two teens only received probation. Charges of rape against the sixth bully, Austin, were dropped. The felony charges had been dropped. The deals were reached with the approval and support of Phoebe's family. Phoebe's family wanted a public apology in court more than they wanted the defendants to serve time.

No adults were ever charged for their negligence regarding Phoebe's persistent bullying, but Phoebe's parents did file a complaint in November 2010 with the Massachusetts Commission Against Discrimination. They asserted the school district did not protect Phoebe from discrimination. The complaint was withdrawn when Phoebe's parents settled with the school district for $225,000.

Phoebe's Legacy

Students are bullied in US schools every day. Research reveals one child is bullied every seven minutes, and 85 percent of the time there is no adult intervention.

In one year, more than 13 million children will be the victims of bullying, with the abuse occurring at school, on the bus, in town, and in cyberspace.

Thirty-four percent of those bullied report bullying happens regularly.[4]

Phoebe Prince's legacy lives on through the attention it has attracted across the country and the world, mobilizing antibullying initiatives. Not only is the issue at the forefront of public discourse, but policy, law, and action have also been prompted to prevent bullying. Officials are reviewing and updating school policies as a result of Phoebe's case and many other cases like hers.

SUICIDE

According to the Centers for Disease Control (CDC), suicide is the third leading cause of death among young people.[5] That means 4,400 people end their own lives purposefully each year. Students who are bullied are five times more likely to turn to suicide than peers who are not bullied.[6] While there is clearly a link between bullying and suicide, research has yet to determine if bullying causes suicide or if those with suicidal tendencies tend to be the target of bullies. The risk factors for both are similar: anxiety, depression, and social withdrawal. And it is not only the victims who entertain thoughts of suicide. Bullies are also more at risk for suicidal thoughts and attempts.

CHAPTER
TWO

WHAT IS BULLYING?

Bullying comes in many forms: being pushed in the school hallway, being called names, getting shoved into a locker, being forced to give up lunch money, being excluded from a group, experiencing physical assaults on the bus, and receiving threatening text messages. Bullying occurs across all grade levels, starting as young as three years old.

Classically, a bully is often thought of as a larger, angry child who is cruel to others who are weaker. Yet a closer look at incidents, bullies, victims, and bystanders reveals bullying is much more complicated. Bullies may actually be popular and likeable.

History of Bullying

Classic literature reveals bullying is not a modern-day phenomenon. *Oliver Twist*, published in 1838 by Charles Dickens, was one of the first novels to focus on the bullying of a child. In Charlotte Brontë's *Jane Eyre* (1847), young Jane is not only bullied by an older cousin

Male bullies are not the only ones who get physical—females can also take part in physical bullying.

but is also punished when she stands up to him. Other novels involving bullying are *Lord of the Flies* (William Golding, 1954), *The Outsiders* (S. E. Hinton, 1967), and the Harry Potter series (J. K. Rowling, 1997–2007). Even dating back to the publication of Dickens's novel, bullying appears to merely be a fact of life.

Accusations of bullying are often met with standard phrases such as "boys will be boys." Another phrase often recited to children to shrug off the effect of taunting is "sticks and stones may break my bones, but words will never hurt me." In the past, bullying has been treated as a rite of passage—something many children must endure and overcome on the way to adulthood.

Then Dan Olweus, a researcher and professor at the University of Bergen in Norway, published a study of bullies and their victims in 1973. His work was the first scientifically based study of its kind, and it revealed

THE MOVIES

Bullying is also a common theme in movies. Frequently, the scenario involves a bullied kid overcoming his or her aggressor or getting out of the bullying situation. Well-known movies such as *The Karate Kid* (1984), *Stand By Me* (1986), *Back to the Future* (1985), *Mean Girls* (2004), and the Harry Potter films (2001–2011) all feature bullies. Throughout, the bullies taunt, tease, push, intimidate, and harass the victims, while audiences root for the victims to develop their own power and win.

the size of the problem in his country. The study helped the public begin to understand bullying as a serious social issue, instead of simply a form of peer conflict. The book was published in the United States in 1978 as *Aggression in the Schools: Bullies and Whipping Boys*.

Armed with his findings, Olweus developed his Bullying Prevention Program, which is aimed at preventing and reducing bullying in schools. After implementing the program in Norway in 1983, Olweus studied its effects, discovering bullying had been reduced by 30 to 50 percent.[1] Since the success of Olweus's program, countless other programs have been developed and brought to schools.

In today's high-tech world, bullying has also evolved to include cyberbullying. Most students now have access to cell phones, computers, tablets, and the like and are now using them as another means to bully others.

Definition of Bullying

In light of the growing awareness of bullying as a social problem, the definition of bullying has been expanded and refined. Today, the American Psychological Association defines bullying as "a form of aggressive behavior in which someone intentionally and repeatedly causes another person injury or discomfort."[2]

Acts of bullying are intentional. The bully purposefully seeks out a victim with the goal of causing harm. In addition, to be considered bullying, the acts of aggression must be repeated over time instead of one-time disagreements or fights.

Another aspect of a full definition of bullying is an imbalance of power. A bully uses his or her physical or social power to inflict harm or cruelty on someone else. The bully can act alone or with a group against a single child.

WHAT BULLYING IS NOT

Not all conflict between peers is bullying. In fact, conflict and learning how to cope with conflict are normal parts of interacting with others. When peers with equal power have a disagreement, this is not bullying. Further, for behavior to be considered bullying, it must be repeated, negative, and purposeful. In normal peer conflicts, children will show remorse and attempt to solve the problem. But in a bullying situation, there is little emotion or problem solving on the bully's part.

Types of Bullying

The stereotypical image of bullying is that of a larger child picking on or harming a smaller child in the school yard. This type of aggression toward a person or his or her possessions is physical bullying. It can involve pushing, hitting, kicking, spitting, tripping, throwing food, defacing someone's property, and more. Shutting someone in a locker or stealing one's clothes in a locker room are also examples of physical bullying.

Another form of bullying is verbal, which uses either spoken or written words. Teasing and name-calling are the most prevalent, but verbal bullying also includes threatening, taunting, or mocking someone else. Rude hand gestures are also a form of bullying. Social bullying is gossiping, excluding the victim, spreading rumors, embarrassing the victim, setting the victim up to take the blame for something, and socially rejecting the victim.

Finally, sexual bullying is another type of victimization. It occurs physically, verbally, or socially

RACISM AND BULLYING

Racial bullying occurs when a bully targets someone based on his or her race or country of origin, and the bully acts based on racist attitudes. This type of bullying may be a result of children learning discrimination against a certain group of people. Children hear and repeat racial slurs and mimic prejudiced behavior. Or, a child may recognize someone of a different race as different and not part of his or her own social group, leading the bully to think the other person is not worthy of respect. While research on the relationship between race and bullying and the rates of such bullying is limited, harassment based on race or ethnicity is covered under federal civil rights laws.

Social bullying includes making someone feel rejected or unwanted.

and happens to both females and males. Girls who are
victims of verbal sexual bullying are subjected to taunts
objectifying their bodies or demeaning their sexuality.
Sexual jokes or threats are also forms of sexual bullying.
So are remarks about a girl's body or comments about
her sexual activity or lack thereof. Physical sexual
bullying is unwanted sexual contact of any kind, such
as bra snapping, pinching, groping, pulling up skirts,
and other unwanted contact. US culture often dictates
that girls act and dress femininely, while boys are
prescribed to be macho and strong. When boys are the

victims of sexual bullying, the attacks are often aimed at the boy's masculinity.

Sexual bullying also happens to those who are of nontraditional sexual orientation, often stemming from homophobia. Homophobic phrases are often used to undermine a boy's masculinity or a girl's femininity. The 2009 National School Climate Survey of lesbian, gay, bisexual, transgender, and questioning (LGBTQ) youth found 85 percent of LGBTQ youth had been verbally bullied in school, and 40 percent had experienced physical harassment due to their sexual identity.[3]

Bullying most often occurs when there is little adult supervision or in situations in which the bully can stay under

BULLYING GENDER DIFFERENCES

While both boys and girls report being the victim of every kind of bullying, statistics reveal boys and girls generally experience different kinds of bullying. Overall, girls spend much more time socializing, while boys engage in more physical activities. This translates into the type of bullying girls experience. Girls tend to bully and be bullied by groups. This social, relational bullying excludes the victim. Boys are bullied by other boys in both physical and emotional ways. Girls report being the victim of sexual bullying more often than boys. Further, girls who reach puberty before their peers are more likely to be targets, as are boys who mature later than peers. In cyberspace, both boys and girls report similar rates of victimization.

Bullies often target victims on their trips to and from school, on the sidewalk, or on the school bus, where little to no adult supervision is present.

the radar. It occurs in school hallways, bathrooms, lunchrooms, locker rooms, and playgrounds. Bullying is also more likely to happen in schools without an effective antibullying policy or in schools in which bullying is an accepted cultural norm. Outside of school, bullies can strike in parks, at the mall, or at someone else's house. There is no reprieve for the bullied even at home. With the evolution of cyberbullying, victims are even bullied in cyberspace.

IT'S A GIRL'S WORLD

In the 2004 documentary *It's a Girl's World*, a 10-year-old girl explains how the bullying between girls feels: "Kind of like imagine like a knife or something; and they just give you those eyes and the knife just goes right through you."[4] The documentary itself explores how girls use friendships as weapons to bully one another through whispering, shunning, and mean looks. "The point is to make the other person feel bad and make yourself feel better," explains another girl. "You feel more powerful. But like sometimes you feel worse."[5] Makers of the documentary sought to expose the cruel and often devastating nature of the relationships that can occur between girls. They wanted to help people recognize that such social bullying should not be the cultural norm.

CHAPTER THREE

CYBERBULLYING

Technology is an integral part of the modern world. People shop, communicate, study, research, play games, watch movies, catch up on the news, and more every day through a myriad of high-tech gadgets. Most students use a cell phone (83 percent of 10- to 18-year-olds, according to a 2010 study by the Cyberbullying Research Center).[1] Text messaging, instant messaging, e-mailing, and social networking are also common. Yet despite its usefulness and appeal, technology has also inadvertently created a new venue for bullies.

Defining Cyberbullying

The first known use of the word *cyberbullying* was in 2000. The definition is still developing since both cyberbullying and technology are evolving. Nonetheless, the Cyberbullying Research Center defines cyberbullying as "when someone repeatedly harasses, mistreats, or makes fun of another person online or

Technology has provided another avenue for bullies to target and attack their victims.

HIGH-TECH SOLUTIONS

One way to combat cyberbullying includes smartphone apps. Some apps monitor students' online usage and supply easier methods for reporting cyberbullying on social networking sites. Other systems support the bullied (by outlining coping strategies), their bullies (by encouraging would-be bullies to stop and think before engaging in cyberbullying), and bystanders (by calling on witnesses to defend the victim). The more complex strategies are currently under construction at the Massachusetts Institute of Technology. There, students are developing systems to detect bullying language. The students have a significant database of offensive statements commonly made by bullies. If a bully attempts to post such comments, the algorithm will identify the language and a message will pop up asking the bully if he or she really wants to send the message.

while using cell phones or other electronic devices."[2] As with any type of bullying, cyberbullying has at its core an intent to cause harm, an imbalance of power, and repeated victimization.

Cyberbullies use instant messaging, e-mailing, and text messaging to send threatening and harassing messages to their victims. Social networking sites such as Facebook and Instagram are other venues for cyberbullies. Perpetrators post false, harmful information about others, or sometimes they gain access to another's profile to make posts as if they were that individual. Bullies belittle their victims in chat rooms. Bash boards are yet another cyberspace location for bullies. The bully creates an online bulletin board about his or her victims where others can then join in making cruel posts. Other means of cyberbullying are through blogs, websites, and Internet games.

How Is Cyberbullying Different?

Cyberbullying clearly differs from its traditional counterpart. Most notably, cyberbullying does not take place face-to-face. This allows for youth who may have little power in face-to-face confrontations to wield a great deal of power in cyberspace. Moreover, being anonymous grants more power, allowing the cyberbully to do things he or she would not ordinarily do because there is little threat of punishment or social consequences. In addition, due to the distance between the bully and the victim, the bully cannot see the reaction of his or her target and thus cannot observe the full extent of the harm he or she is inflicting.

For victims, cyberbullying can be more humiliating than traditional bullying. Pictures, taunts, rumors, and the like can all be revisited and forwarded publically millions of times. To make matters worse, messages, photos, or videos often cannot be taken off the Internet. This means the victimization can go on indefinitely, and the victim often believes everyone knows about it. The

Just as bullies can use the Internet as a weapon, victims can use it as a means of emotional support. At a primary school in Scotland, students began the campaign Support Me to raise awareness of and combat cyberbullying. Since then, it has grown into a company for kids run by kids. Their slogan is, "If you ever feel you're stuck in a deep black hole, we're the shining light at the end of the tunnel."[4] The group of students runs workshops, shares information about cyberbullying, and offers advice about how to stay safe online. They sell the resources they develop, as well as wristbands and other merchandise with antibullying messages.

bullying can occur 24 hours a day, seven days a week, and all year long.

Types of Cyberbullying

When 14-year-old Amanda Marcuson reported some eighth grade girls for stealing a pencil case with makeup in it, the girls retaliated in cyberspace. At home, Amanda was subjected to dozens of instant messages calling her a "liar" and a "stuck-up bitch."[3] In all, she received more than 50 increasingly unpleasant messages. This type of harassment is a common form of cyberbullying. Cyber harassment occurs when a bully repeatedly sends hateful messages to his or her victim. This is done via e-mail, cell phones, or social networking sites.

Cyberbullying can be viewed worldwide, sometimes making this type of bullying even more difficult to endure than traditional bullying.

Cyberstalking takes harassment one step further. As with physical stalking, cyberstalking is the act of following someone, often secretly, online. Usually the bully intends to harass, but the behavior also includes threats. In Florida, as many as 15 girls cyberstalked 12-year-old Rebecca Ann Sedwick for almost a year. Rebecca constantly received messages saying, "You should die," and "Why don't you go kill yourself."[5] The cyberstalking did not stop even after Rebecca's mother began homeschooling her.

FELONY CHARGES FOR BULLIES IN SEDWICK CASE

Twelve-year-old Rebecca Ann Sedwick was relentlessly stalked and harassed online for almost a year. The cyberbullying sent Rebecca into depression, and in September 2013 she could not stand it any longer. She took her own life. The investigation that followed revealed the bullying endured by Rebecca was not simply teen cruelty. In the mind of Polk County Sheriff Grady Judd, the bullying was, in fact, criminal harassment. As a result, two girls, ages 14 and 12, were charged with stalking. The charges were eventually dropped, but the case was an example that minors could be charged for cyberbullying.

Attacking someone's character or criticizing them online is another type of cyberbullying. This type of bullying goes to the heart of a person's image, and the disrespectful, false information damages a person's reputation. The bully may start rumors, call names, or threaten the victim. This type of bullying may also involve posting photos the victim wanted kept private or posting altered photos portraying the victim in embarrassing ways.

Some cyberbullies impersonate their victims to inflict harm. In these cases, the bully poses as another individual online. This can be done by using the victim's password to gain access to his or her accounts or simply by creating accounts under the victim's name. The bully then uses the victim's account to communicate inappropriate, cruel, and inflammatory information as if he or she were the victim. In one case, a Massachusetts ninth grader finally told his mother when other students claimed he was saying nasty things about others on Facebook. The boy himself did not have a Facebook account, but his mother discovered one had been set up in his name, complete with a profile picture of her son. His wall contained scathing remarks about classmates who ultimately began to reject the boy, even though he had nothing to do with it. There are countless other ways bullies use cyberspace to victimize others, such as trickery, happy slapping, online polls, text wars, and outing—the act of making someone's personal information public.

The Challenges

Cyberbullying is a growing issue due to the increasing use of technology. Combating it presents its own set of challenges. Many people believe cyberbullying is not a problem or consider it harmless. Because

HAPPY SLAPPING

One form of cyberbullying is happy slapping. A bully physically assaults his or her target while someone captures the bullying on video or takes pictures. The pictures or video are then posted online for the world to see. The bullies often attack in groups and find humor in what they see as a prank, thus the term *happy slapping*.

Cyberbullies can attack their victims anywhere, even at home.

of the explosion of technology since the turn of the century, parents and law enforcement are struggling to understand who should take responsibility for online behavior. Parents are frequently not as tech savvy as their children; schools are hesitant to intervene in online activity originating off-campus; and the law is also hesitant to become involved unless someone's safety is at risk. Another challenge in stopping cyberbullying is the fact that many victims do not tell their parents what is going on because the victims fear losing their cell phones or online privileges.

But no matter the challenge, research shows cyberbullying is an issue. In a 2010 study, the Cyberbullying Research Center found more than 20 percent of students surveyed had been cyberbullied at some point in their life, and about the same number reported being the bully.[6]

FREE SPEECH

At the center of the controversy around punishment for cyberbullying is the First Amendment of the US Constitution, which guarantees individuals the right to free speech. One of the first federal cases to be heard regarding cyber behavior and the First Amendment, *Beussink v. Woodland R-IV School District,* occurred in 1998. The court had to consider whether a school could punish a student for speech posted on the Internet from an off-campus computer. The student had created a website, on his own time, condemning school officials. He also called for students to voice their opinions about the principal's performance running the school. The school initially disciplined the student. The student, however, took his case to court. Ultimately, the court found that by punishing the student, the school had violated the student's First Amendment rights. The court held that the website did not create a disturbance at school and did not violate any civil rights. This notable case was the first federal case in which the court had to confront the issue of free speech rights, school accountability, and online behavior. The case helped lay groundwork for subsequent cyberbullying cases.

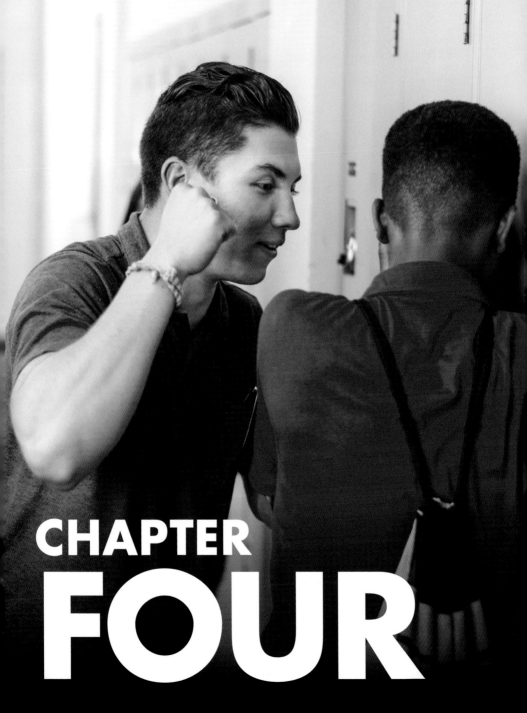

CHAPTER FOUR

THE BULLY

Bullies are typically portrayed as stocky males who loom over their peers. In addition, the stereotype often portrays bullies as sullen loners. The reality, however, is much different. Bullies often have many friends who empower them and validate their actions.

While there is no single profile fitting all bullies, research has shown bullies do, in fact, share some common characteristics. Most notably, bullies tend to have dominant personalities and use force to assert themselves. In addition, many bullies are aggressive, impulsive, tough, and short-tempered. They may have trouble following rules and are more likely to purposefully break the rules. Bullies have a more positive attitude toward violence than others, and they show little empathy for the bullied or guilt for their actions. Bullies enjoy the reward of overpowering others and view bullying as fun.

Studies also show bullies report being less depressed, anxious, and lonely than their classmates. Peers

Bullies come in all sizes, races, and genders.

frequently see bullies as having a high social status or at least a small group of friends. Likewise, teachers frequently report bullies are popular in school.

Types of Bullies

One type of bully is the one who uses physical bullying to victimize others. These bullies fit the stereotype of the kid who steals lunch money and pushes other kids around. Another type of bully is the manipulative social bully who is often part of the popular crowd.

ARE WE TOO QUICK TO CRY BULLY?

Researchers are beginning to question the use of the word *bullying*. As reports of suicide as a result of bullying increasingly hit the headlines, school staff, parents, and lawmakers recognize the immediate need to address the bullying issue. Yet in doing so, everything today is labeled bullying, whereas not nearly as much was labeled bullying 25 years ago. According to some, this knee-jerk reaction to slap the bullying label on every fight and every tease is overly reactionary. They argue this actually undermines incidents in which true bullying has occurred. Elizabeth Englander, an expert on aggression, says, "The label 'bullying' is really incendiary. It ratchets everything up emotionally. It makes it hard to really address, rationally, what the best course of action is."[1]

In fact, there are many cases of isolated, aggressive, hurtful behavior that are not bullying. These are opportunities for students to learn to deal with minor conflict. Experts are calling for a more precise use of the word instead of reactive labeling so parents, students, and school staff can focus on the best way to handle each incident.

Social bullies purposely exclude victims from their activities and discussions.

These bullies tend to strike through social bullying by using taunts, gossip, and exclusion of their victims. The newest type of bully is the cyberbully who uses the Internet to harass, stalk, embarrass, and otherwise victimize others.

Another type of bully is the bully victim. Children in this category have been victims, yet turn to bullying in retaliation. Kids who are bullied and then become the bully are systematically rejected by peers and pushed into reacting. They are characterized as students with poor self-control, learning difficulties, or behavior problems. They are often kids with whom peers have trouble associating. These unpopular kids are also more likely to have deep psychological issues and depression because they are both the bully and the victim.

Both Genders Bully

Both boys and girls engage in bully behavior, but boys tend to use more direct physical and verbal behaviors than girls. When looking at male bullies, studies show they bully both boys and girls and are just as likely as girls to use social and emotional taunting. Female bullying can be just as aggressive as male bullying; however, the tactics are more indirect, such as damaging relationships, spreading rumors, and excluding the victim. More than boys, girls tend to bully in groups and attack within a

MEAN GIRLS

Bullying is increasing in younger children. Girls as young as three or four years old are both victims and bullies. These bullies exclude others, purposely damage another's friendships, and try to get the victim in trouble with adults. In 2002, two books were published exposing the mean girl phenomena. *Odd Girl Out* by Rachel Simmons shined light on how harmful female bullying can be. Also, in *Queen Bees and Wannabes* by Rosalind Wiseman, mean girls were followed throughout the school day, exposing their bullying.

group of friends to inflict maximum psychological hurt. Research suggests physical bullying among girls is on the rise.

Studies also indicate girls are more likely than boys to engage in cyberbullying. Rates of cyberbullying vary depending on the study and how cyberbullying is defined. The method of bullying also varies. Girls report spreading rumors and harassing, while boys admit to posting hurtful pictures or videos.

Why Do People Bully?

There are multiple reasons people bully. Those who bully have physical, social, or other forms of power and do not know how to handle it. Studies have also concluded bullying is a learned behavior, and thus environmental factors can lead to bullying. Home, school, and community environments play a particularly large role in the behavior of bullies. Bearing witness to aggressive behavior and domestic violence in the home or community teaches kids aggression is normal and strategies they can use to become bullies themselves. They are also more likely than peers to be abused at home or to have unpredictable parents. Finally, if a child constantly receives negative feedback, he or she tends

Frequent exposure to domestic violence can lead children to bullying because it gives them the false perception violence is normal and acceptable.

to turn to negative behaviors in order to gain power and attention. Bullies tend to have friends who value aggression and violence and who encourage aggressive behavior.

School culture likewise plays a role in a bully's behavior. Larger schools and schools with large class sizes report more bullying due to poor supervision. In addition, schools with accepting or indifferent attitudes about bullying and poor supervision are more likely to experience bullying issues. In some schools, bullying or hazing are almost a part of the school culture.

Another factor leading kids to bully is the reward. Bullying behavior often results in material gain, such as when a victim hands over lunch

HAZING

Incoming freshman, rookie teammates, and kids joining various clubs are often subjected to initiation rituals, known as hazing. Hazing is the practice of forcing someone to take part in embarrassing or dangerous activities. For many, this hazing is a rite of passage, carried out to develop camaraderie between students in a group or on a team. However, many acts of hazing involve humiliation, harassment, or even physical abuse. Despite this, incidences of hazing are generally shrugged off as something that happens all the time and as no big deal.

The effect of such dismissal of humiliation, harassment, and abuse is a cultural acceptance of bullying. And, far from creating camaraderie, hazing can create mistrust and isolation, and it can negatively affect relationships between teammates or group members. In the individual, hazing often induces stress and anxiety and leads to poor self-esteem.

THE ROLE OF MEDIA IN BULLYING

It is clear children mimic behaviors learned in the world around them. Violence in movies, video games, and on television is a risk factor for children to become bullies. Tracy Vaillancourt, a specialist in children's mental health and violence prevention at the University of Ottawa states, "The research literature on aggression is very clear that with [aggression], it's monkey see, monkey do."[2]

In addition, experiments have revealed that when children are shown a violent media clip or play a violent video game, their behavior immediately afterward is typically more aggressive. And, those children who are routinely exposed to media violence are more likely to be more aggressive than their peers. While media alone may not be responsible for a child's aggressive behavior, it is definitely a factor that warrants concern.

money or possessions; social gain from the assumed respect of bystanders; or the release of pent-up frustration or anger. In cases of cyberbullying, bullies are more prone to act because they can remain anonymous. In some cases, the cyberbully adopts a meaner, more spiteful personality online than he or she would in person. The cyberbully is also less likely to be caught and does not have to deal with the victim face-to-face. Other reasons people cyberbully include boredom, retaliation for being bullied, and a want for attention.

Schools, parents, researchers, and law enforcement are learning the risk factors leading children to become bullies. Not only will this help reduce bully behavior, but it will help the bullies themselves. Left unchecked, children who bully are more likely to engage in increasingly antisocial and deviant behavior as they age, and they are more likely to have a criminal record as an adult.

NO LABELS

As parents, educators, and lawmakers deal with bullying behavior, experts warn they must be careful not to label kids. The label of *bully* can be difficult and damaging and have long-term effects on a child. Instead of labeling the child, parents and educators should label the child's behavior. Using a label sends the message that the child's behavior does not change or will not improve over time. Calling a child a bully can also affect the child's self-image, as well as how others perceive him or her. This leads to prejudgment of the child as opposed to giving support to the child to change. Finally, there are many factors feeding into a child's behavior that should be considered. Similarly, experts warn against labeling kids as victims. The focus for both bullies and victims should be on behavior, not labels.

CHAPTER
FIVE

THE BULLIED

According to the CDC Youth Risk Behavior Surveillance in 2011, 20.1 percent of US students reported being bullied at school within one year of the survey.[1] That is one in every five children. In total, Caucasian students reported being bullied more than Hispanic or African-American students.[2] In cyberspace, 16.2 percent of students nationwide reported being the victim of cyberbullying, with females reporting being bullied more than males.[3]

Who They Are

Victims come from all social classes, races, and genders. They can be kids who just do not fit in. Or maybe they are bullied because of their physical appearance or mannerisms. These children tend to be quiet, sensitive, anxious, or insecure. Male victims are generally smaller than their peers and avoid confrontation. These are passive victims.

The bullied, or victims, may be either quiet and insecure or loud and aggressive.

BULLYING IN THE NFL

Can a 312-pound (142 kg) National Football League (NFL) lineman be bullied? November 2013 news headlines reveal the answer is yes. During football season, offensive lineman Jonathan Martin left the Miami Dolphins as a result of ongoing harassment from teammates. Martin, who is African American, was the victim of repeated bullying by another lineman, Richie Incognito, who is Caucasian. Incognito had sent vulgar, abusive, threatening, and racist text messages to Martin. According to some, the racial slurs in the messages were not isolated incidents but were instead words Incognito frequently used. The Miami Dolphins suspended Incognito indefinitely, and sources assert his time on the team is over. As of December 2013, the NFL investigation of the matter was still pending.

There are also bully victims. These children are immature, impulsive, irritable, and easily provoked by the bully. When they fight back in a bullying situation, the bully will manipulate the situation to make it seem as if the provocative victim was the bully. These students are called bully victims. The bully victims not only have some of the social and emotional problems of passive victims, but they also tend to have the behavior problems of bullies.

There are certain factors putting children at risk for being bullied. Most notably, children perceived as different are often bullied. They are tormented because of their weight, the clothes or glasses they wear, and other such factors. Children viewed by peers as weak, depressed, or unconfident are also at risk. Less popular children, as well as those who do not get along well with others, or those who have recently moved into the community, may be targets. Naturally, there are exceptions to this, wherein not all children with these traits will be bullied and not all children who are bullied will have these risk factors.

Research has also begun to show certain groups of children are at risk for being bullied. These groups include children with learning disabilities such as attention deficit hyperactivity disorder (ADHD), chronically ill children, and children with physical difficulties such as cerebral palsy, muscular dystrophy, obesity, and partial paralysis. Children who are chronically ill are at higher risk because they often miss school due to their illnesses. Repeated absences interfere with their ability to make friends, which puts them at risk for bullying. Another targeted group is LGBTQ youth. This has become an area of increasing concern. Reports reveal nine out of ten LGBTQ students have been the targets of bullying.[4]

Warning Signs

Since most victims of bullying keep the abuse to themselves, parents and friends need to be aware of the warning signs:

- Isolation and withdrawal from social interactions at school and at home

- A drop in grades and lack of interest in school and school activities, including skipping classes or faking an illness to avoid going to school

- Taking a different route to school or seeking another mode of transportation

- Nightmares, insomnia, or bed-wetting

- Unexplainable scratches, bruises, or torn clothing, as well as damaged or missing possessions

- Uncontrolled, unpredictable anger and irritability

- Nervousness, anxiety, worry, and crying

- Lack of self-confidence

LGBTQ teens are two to three times more likely
to be bullied than their straight peers.

- Changes in behavior, such as self-injuring, drug and alcohol use, a change in appearance, becoming overly aggressive, and sudden interest in violent media

Children who are cyberbullied may show some of the above warning signs, but there may be other signs in their use of technology. For example, it may be a sign something is wrong if the child suddenly stops using his or her cell phone or computer. Another warning

JOE'S WALK FOR CHANGE

Jadin Bell was one of the bullied. At age 15, he took his own life after relentless bullying. He was targeted both at school and online for being gay. In his honor, his father embarked on a journey to walk from Oregon to New York, called Joe's Walk for Change. He wanted to spread the word about his son, acceptance, and the evils of bullying. His goal was to save at least one child's life by educating parents, kids, teachers, and anyone else who would listen. In Colorado, Lincoln County Sheriff Tom Nestor met Joe Bell on his trek. Nestor later expressed Bell's impact: "This man had to [have] made a huge difference in everyone he met. He made me realize how important basic humanity still is. I will pass his story on to many people."5

Sadly, Nestor was called out to a report of a pedestrian hit and killed on a rural highway. The deceased pedestrian was Joe Bell. In honor of both Jadin and Joe, Joe's Walk for Change continues on its mission to "[change] the way people communicate, [end] the stigma of suicide, and [fight] for equal rights for everyone."6 The goal is to continue to raise awareness about bullying, suicide, and gay youth through "likes" on Facebook, raising money, and walking a portion of Joe's proposed route.

sign is if the use of a cell phone causes a student to be nervous, anxious, or depressed. Finally, some cyberbully victims become secretive about their computer or cell phone use.

Why They Keep It a Secret

In the months prior to March 2001, Elizabeth Bush was mercilessly taunted by a group of girls. Elizabeth was ostracized to the point where she took a gun to school and shot one of the girls, who was a former friend, in the shoulder. At Elizabeth's arraignment, her father said, "We had no way of knowing how much she was taunted."[7]

One of the biggest reasons children do not tell anyone about being bullied is shame. Bullying can make children feel worthless and isolated. Boys often feel the pressure of cultural expectations to just take

DEAR BULLY

In an effort to raise awareness about bullying, top authors and editors of books for teens and children have come together to share their stories. The result is the website DearBully.com and the 2011 book *Dear Bully*. In the book, 70 well-known authors relate their experiences about being bullied. Authors include Lauren Oliver (*New York Times* bestselling author of *Before I Fall* and more), R. L. Stine (author of the popular Goosebumps series), Carolyn Mackler (author of Printz Honor Book *The Earth, My Butt, and Other Big Round Things* and other books), and many others.

Boys are often less likely to report bullying than girls because of shame.

it and deal with the bullying on their own. There is a great deal of disgrace in not being able to stand up for oneself or deal with problems on one's own. The bullied also keep the secret out of fear of retaliation from the bully. Whether the threats are real or implied makes no difference—the bullied often stay quiet.

Bullying also tends to further isolate kids, which in turn leads them to believe no one can help them or is willing to help them. The bullying is so overpowering the bullied feel they are alone. Moreover, students may have witnessed situations when adults were made aware of bullying but nothing was done.

SIBLING BULLYING

A 2013 study published by the American Academy of Pediatrics reported bullying among siblings should not be dismissed as normal sibling rivalry.[8] As more and more attention is given to peer bullying, so too should attention be given to sibling bullying. The study looked at actions typically deemed "normal," such as stealing a sibling's belongings, calling names, physically assaulting, and the like. Researchers discovered a distinct correlation between the level of sibling aggression and the mental health of the victim. Children who had experienced mild to severe aggression reported poor mental health and distress. Researchers concluded, just as with peer bullying, sibling aggression is potentially harmful to the victim.

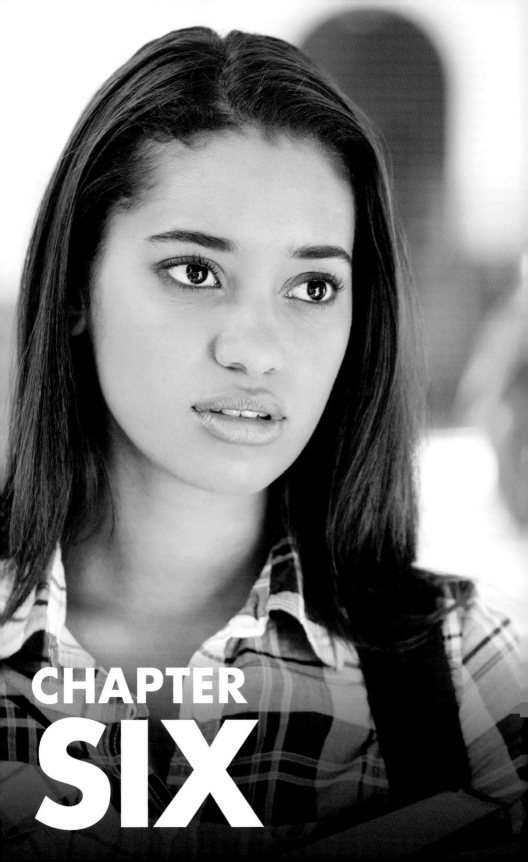

CHAPTER
SIX

THE BYSTANDER

In a bullying situation, a bystander is someone who is near the bullying and may not be directly taking part in it. As innocent and uninvolved as this may sound, being a bystander is not quite as simple as it seems.

Freshman Tyler Clementi was secretly videotaped by his roommate Dharun Ravi at Rutgers University, New Jersey, in 2010. In the video, Tyler was on a date with a man. Ravi invited others to join in watching the live streaming of the date. Countless individuals in the dorm and online joined in watching the live feed. Not only did no one step in to stop Ravi, but students forwarded the information to others. No one met with authorities to report what had happened either. And not one bystander helped Tyler cope with his humiliation after he found out his relations were made public. Tyler ultimately ended his own life.

Bystanders are the third party in the bullying triad. Bystanders contribute to bullying even if they are not directly involved. Pioneering bullying researcher

Disengaged onlookers are bystanders who witness bullying but choose not to get involved.

THE BYSTANDER EFFECT

One reason bullying bystanders do not intervene can be explained, in part, by the bystander effect. The phrase *bystander effect* was coined after the attack and murder of a young woman, Kitty Genovese, in New York in 1964. Numerous tenants of the nearby building witnessed the attack, but no one came to her aid or called the police. Social psychologists describe the bystander effect as "when the presence of others hinders an individual from intervening in an emergency situation."[1] The effect occurs partly because people believe someone else will do something. The more witnesses there are, the less likely someone will take action. The bystander effect can also be attributed to the influence of the social group. Students may look to others around them to determine how to act. This can be especially dangerous in places where school culture accepts bully behavior and little is done to prevent it.

Dan Olweus identified these bystanders and what they do when bullying occurs. He defined different roles as part of a "bullying circle." The first role is the child who initiates and actively engages in bullying. Next are the bully's "henchmen." These children do not typically plan or initiate any behavior, but they do take an active part in the bullying once it has begun.

The third role is that of supporters. In essence, they take a passive role in the bullying by supporting the bully without actually engaging in the bullying acts themselves. For example, they may cheer on the bully. Next are passive supporters who watch and enjoy the bullying yet do not openly or actively support the bully. The bully circle also includes disengaged onlookers. These students see everything but choose to stay uninvolved. They pretend they do not see the bullying and feel it is not their business. Another type of bystander is someone who sees the bullying and does not like it, yet still chooses not to help. Finally, there are those who choose to not simply be a bystander, but to get involved, either personally or by getting help, to defend the victim. The eighth role Olweus defined in his circle is the target of the bullying: the victim.

LANDMARK CASE IN CANADA

In November 2000, 14-year-old Dawn-Marie Wesley hung herself after being the victim of extreme harassment. For the first time ever in Canada, a judge found one of Dawn-Marie's tormentors guilty of criminal harassment for her aggressive and profane verbal bullying of Dawn-Marie. While the judgment itself was groundbreaking because it held the student accountable for her words, Provincial Court Judge Jill Rounthwaite denounced the schools allowing such bullying to occur. Rounthwaite noted Dawn-Marie's classmates "added to [the] power and intimidation" of the bullies simply by being bystanders and doing nothing. "I was particularly dismayed," Rounthwaite said, "that none of the bystanders had the moral strength or the courage to stand in front of Dawn-Marie Wesley, to tell the bullies to stop, go away, leave her alone."[2] Rounthwaite believes school environments need to change to empower kids to stand up for what is right.

Bystanders who cheer on a bully are considered supporters
even if they do not partake in any physical bullying.

Studies show the great majority of students do not come to the aid of the bullied. In fact, according to a 2004 poll of US students, less than 20 percent of students who witness bullying actually intervene in some way even though the vast majority reported feeling sorry for the victim.[3]

In cyberbullying cases, the roles of the bystanders are similar. Bystanders may egg on a bully, fuel rumors started by bullies, or add hurtful messages to websites or bash boards. Or, a bystander may know about the bullying but choose to say or do nothing to stop it. In other situations, a bully will encourage a bystander with fabricated rumors in an attempt to get the bystander to attack a target.

Parents and teachers play a critical role in bullying and can also be bystanders. Research has shown incidences of bullying are high at schools in which bullying is an accepted part of the school culture. But in schools where teachers and staff play a strong role in bully prevention, reports of bullying decrease. And, just as with any bystander, if adults do not respond to bullying or expect victims to shrug off the bullying, they are approving the bullying behavior.

Why Bystanders Do Not Intervene

There are many reasons bystanders give for not getting involved. Perhaps the most common reason students cite for not stopping the bullying is fear of being hurt themselves. Staying away from bullies is a conscious method of self-preservation. Students do not want to provoke bullies and

In many cases, bystanders are afraid to get involved for fear of becoming another one of the bully's targets.

subject themselves to bullying; nor do they want to risk their status as part of the in-group if they attempt to defend someone on the outside. The bystander risks being labeled a rat or snitch if he or she gets involved or reports bullying.

Bystanders are also less likely to stop the bullying if the bully is a friend. Similarly, a bystander is more likely to help the bullied if the bullied is a friend. Bystanders who are not friends with the victim may feel the situation is not their problem—or that the victim had it coming.

In other situations, students avoid getting involved because they think doing so would only escalate the situation. Finally, often bystanders simply do not know what to do. This happens when students have not been taught how to report bullying or where to go for help.

Unknowingly, bystanders send messages of support to the bully and magnify the humiliation of

Even voiceless bystanders give power to the bully and make the victim feel inferior.

the victim. Olweus believes students must be taught to change roles in the bullying cycle. No matter the role a child has played in the circle, he or she can learn how to move between roles to become an integral part of stopping bullying. This, Olweus says, is key to preventing bullying.

CHAPTER
SEVEN

THE EFFECTS OF BULLYING

Bullying may start in a school hallway or on a playground. Now it even occurs in homes, via the Internet. But it does not end when the incident ends. Instead, the effects of bullying shadow the bully, the bullied, and the bystander as children and into adulthood.

In eighth grade, Joey admitted to a friend he was gay. The friend told other kids, who began to taunt, shun, and threaten Joey. As a result of the bullying, Joey began having nightmares, he gained weight, and he even considered suicide. Luckily for Joey, he was able to change schools.

The effects of bullying on the victim often quickly manifest themselves psychologically, physically, and academically. The emotional toll causes the bullied to become anxious, depressed, and unconfident. Bullied children are also three times more likely to

Bully victims tend to have a drop in academic performance, and some avoid going to school altogether.

get headaches, feel lethargic, and wet the bed. They are two times more likely to report tension, sleep problems, stomach pains, and lack of appetite. Finally, victims of continual bullying are more likely to harm themselves or commit suicide. Cyberbullying has effects similar to traditional bullying. Victims report higher rates of depression, frustration, and anger.

Even bystanders suffer at the hands of the bully. Studies indicate those who witness peers being victimized are more likely to feel anxiety, depression, helplessness, or guilt for not intervening. Bystanders can also be tempted to participate to get on the good side of the bully.

Bullies who have never been stopped are more likely

Bullies are more likely than peers to carry a
weapon and partake in violent behavior.

to get into fights, steal, vandalize, and experiment
with drugs and alcohol. Experts have found bullies are
also prone to break other rules and participate in other
antisocial behavior.

Bullycide

Another effect of bullying is bullycide. The term *bullycide* was coined in a book titled *Bullycide: Death at Playtime* by Neil Marr and Tim Field, published in 2001. Bullycide is when a victim commits suicide because he or she can no longer tolerate the effects of being bullied. Such was the case of 17-year-old Tyler Long. As a child, Tyler was fun loving, social, and enjoyed regular childhood activities such as karate and video games. But then the bullying began. Diagnosed with Asperger's syndrome, a form of autism, Tyler was perceived as different by his peers. His peers used these differences to torment him for years.

Bullies stole Tyler's belongings, spit in his food, and verbally harassed him. His parents reported the bullying to the school as soon as it started but were met with indifference and inaction. Tyler's dad recounted how the bullying stole Tyler's pride and how the boy they once knew disappeared. In October of his junior year, Tyler could not take it anymore. He hung himself. Every day his family continues to deal with the effects bullying had on Tyler. One look at news headlines reveals suicide as a result of bullying is a growing problem, and some studies suggest bullying can be directly related to 30 percent of all suicides.[3]

School Shootings

Another tragic result of bullying is school shootings. In these cases, the bullied retaliates with violence. Research suggests two-thirds of school shooters report being bullied through

SCHOOL ENVIRONMENT

Bullying undoubtedly affects individuals. But it also affects families, communities, and schools. In schools where bullying is part of the culture, the school environment is one of fear. Students worry they will become victims, be rejected, or lose social status. One report stated 20 percent of students carry this fear throughout the school day.[4]

Further, in schools where bullying occurs without appropriate staff intervention, students have difficulty learning and report a dislike for school. Students also feel as though staff members are not in control and do not truly care about them.

After opening fire at his school, Luke Woodham claimed his actions were the result of bullying he had experienced.

threats, harassment, and physical harm.[5] In a 1997 case, 16-year-old Luke Woodham opened fired in his school, killing two classmates and wounding seven others. His reason for the spree was clear in a note: "I am not insane. I am angry. I killed because people like me are mistreated every day."[6] Luke's words are a valuable insight into the minds of many school shooters.

ADULT BULLIES

Bullying does not always end after childhood. An adult bully's goal is to dominate others and win power, just as it is among youth. The workplace is a common place for adult bullying. The actions look much the same as those in childhood and can include ignoring, humiliating, spreading rumors, putting down, and leaving the victim out of social events. Almost 25 percent of US adults report experiencing some kind of bullying at work.[8]

Effects into Adulthood

For many victims of bullying, the effects last into adulthood. Olweus conducted and published a study in 1993 of young men who were bullied in junior high school. His findings revealed the bullied were still likely to suffer from depression and low self-esteem even a decade after the bullying ended.[7] Other research has shown adults who were bullied as children are more anxious overall and have difficulty in social situations. For some adults, the effects of bullying led to trust issues, trouble holding down a job, and agoraphobia, a fear of being helpless in an embarrassing situation.

A 2013 study revealed bully victims show the greatest detrimental effects into adulthood. The study looked into the impact of bullying on all those exposed to bullying—victims, the bullies, and bully victims. Results revealed bully victims were "over six times more likely to be diagnosed with a serious illness, smoke regularly, or develop a psychiatric disorder compared to those not involved in bullying."[9] This is due in part to the fact that these individuals are socially defeated because not only were they bullied, but they fought back and were unsuccessful. Other factors include poor coping skills, mental health problems, or an inability to regulate one's emotions.

Students labeled as bullies have a greater likelihood of depression, anxiety, and substance abuse as adults. They are also more likely to have a criminal record. As many as 60 percent of adults who were identified as bullies between grades six and nine had at least one criminal conviction by age 24.[10] The aggressive behaviors also tend to escalate into more extreme violence and sexual harassment as the bully ages. As a result, many bullies are unable to sustain positive relationships.

They may also be abusive toward coworkers, spouses, and their own children. With such detrimental effects resulting from bullying, action to prevent it becomes imperative.

THE FINANCIAL COST OF BULLYING

Bullying also comes with a financial price tag. Pervasive bullying creates a negative school environment. As a result, schools see an increase in suspensions, skipping school, and alternative school placements. Most schools receive money based on average daily attendance. Thus, in schools with high absence rates, reimbursement is less, often totaling tens of thousands of dollars in a school year. The effects of bullying also extend beyond school hallways. Those who experience bullying are more likely to have health-care costs, be involved with the justice system, and access social services programs.

Yet fostering a positive school environment also comes at a cost. In order to effectively implement antibullying programs, schools must devote both time and resources. The Olweus Bullying Prevention Program, for example, costs $7.70 per student per year to implement. Beginning in 2006, the Highmark Foundation funded an initiative to implement the program into dozens of Pennsylvania schools. The results showed a clear reduction in bullying across all grade levels for several years. While assessing the cost-benefit of the program's implementation is complex, the analysis revealed if only two students were prevented from transferring to another school because of bullying, the cost of the program is recovered. Health-care and societal costs were also reduced, further highlighting the benefits of effective antibullying programs in schools.

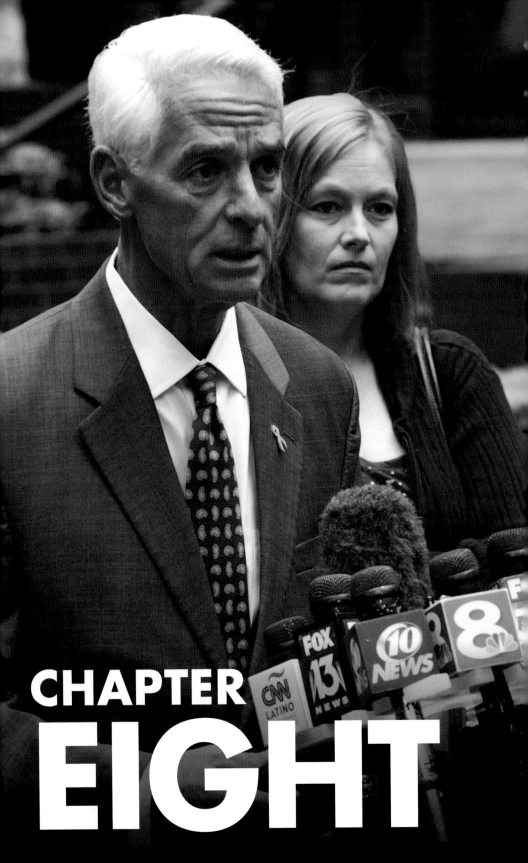

CHAPTER
EIGHT

LEGISLATION

As of December 2013, 49 states in the United States had antibullying laws. Montana was the only state without such a law. Forty-seven states include electronic harassment in their antibullying laws and 18 specifically use the word *cyberbullying*. As of 2013, there was no federal law prohibiting bullying in schools or defining criminal penalties for cyberbullying.

The first antibullying legislation was enacted in 1999. In April of that year, two student shooters at Columbine High School took the lives of 12 students and one teacher. It was the first nationally visible incident involving student shooters who were presumed to be long-time victims of bullying. In the wake of that tragedy, legislators began to take action. Georgia was the first state to pass antibullying legislation, requiring schools to address bullying and foster prevention through educational programs.

Between 1999 and 2010, more than 120 new bills were enacted by states nationwide. These bills either

In October 2013, former Florida governor Charlie Crist spoke about the need to protect youth from cyberbullying as Tricia Norman, the mother of Rebecca Sedwick, looks on.

introduced or updated statutes related to bullying. Many defined bullying and related behaviors more clearly and outlined policies prohibiting such behavior in schools. Yet in each of the 49 states with antibullying laws, the specifics vary widely. The majority of laws require states to create bullying policies and to implement training for staff and education for students. As of summer 2013, many states had proposed laws to include cyberbullying and/or electronic harassment as well as off-campus behavior.

One aspect of antibullying legislation involves defining both bullying and harassment. Many of the new laws enacted since 1999 were modeled after existing laws about civil rights and even used some of the same language from those laws.

Early Cases

The Fourteenth Amendment of the US Constitution protects all citizens from discrimination based on race, sex, nationality,

MEGAN MEIER CYBERBULLYING PREVENTION ACT

The first attempt to pass federal cyberbullying legislation was introduced in April 2009. The Megan Meier Cyberbullying Prevention Act was intended to outline penalties for those who use "electronic means to support severe, repeated, and hostile behavior."[1] Opponents feared the bill would infringe on First Amendment rights and was not specific enough in defining cyberbullying. The act did not become law.

In the 1990s, for the first time, the Fourteenth Amendment protected a gay person as Jamie Nabozny fought for equal rights and protection against bullying.

or religion. In 1993, Jamie Nabozny became the first gay student to invoke protection under the Fourteenth Amendment. At the time, Jamie was a 17-year-old student who had suffered years of bullying by peers. He was often called homophobic names. Bullies knocked books out of his hands and routinely pushed and tripped him in school hallways. The physical abuse worsened, and the acts against him became more heinous. School administrators did nothing to protect Jamie, even after incidents were brought to their attention.

Ultimately, Jamie ran away and at last connected with a gay and lesbian organization. He also found a lawyer who helped him sue the school district. Their suit claimed Jamie had been denied equal rights because the school failed to help him because he was gay. The second part of the claim stated the school discriminated against Jamie because it did not punish Jamie's tormentors for sexual harassment when it would have done so if the harassment had been against a girl. The lawyers had to prove the school officials were aware of the severe, relentless nature of the bullying yet remained indifferent. In July 1996, a federal court outlined the responsibility of schools to protect gay students. The case was sent back to a lower court where it had originally been rejected. The jury found the school officials were indeed accountable for not putting an end to the antigay bullying against Jamie. The school district settled for approximately $900,000 plus medical expenses.

In addition to using the Fourteenth Amendment, other students have turned to Title IX for protection. Part of the Education Amendments of 1972, Title IX prohibits sexual discrimination or harassment in any educational facility receiving federal funds. In 1994, fifth-grader LaShonda Davis's family used Title IX to bring a sexual discrimination and harassment lawsuit against her school district. For months, LaShonda was sexually harassed, both physically and verbally, by a boy in her school. Despite the fact school staff knew of the harassment LaShonda endured, they did nothing to intervene.

On May 24, 1999, the Supreme Court ruled schools were liable for protecting students from sexual harassment. Regarding the case, Justice Sandra Day O'Connor stated schools would be held responsible

SAFE SCHOOLS IMPROVEMENT ACT OF 2013

In March 2013, the Safe Schools Improvement Act was introduced in the House of Representatives. The act would "address and take action to prevent bullying and harassment of students."[2] It was introduced after Congress found, among other things, bullying creates a negative school environment; causes physical, psychological, and academic harm; and that interventions to address bullying and harassment are successful in reducing such behavior and improving a school's environment. It also specifically includes cyberbullying.

LaShonda Davis's mother Aurelia, *left*, and father, *center*, watch as their attorney, *at microphone*, speaks to reporters after Aurelia's lawsuit of sexual harassment of her daughter.

for being indifferent to harassment interfering with a student's education. Further, the US Department of Education explained Title IX could be used by gay students for protection against harassment. Today, Title IX is more specifically defined, prohibiting all sex-based discrimination, "including sexual harassment, harassment based on a student's failure to conform to gender stereotypes, and sexual assault."[3]

Cyberbullying

Lawmakers continue grappling with how to define cyberbullying. They are also attempting to establish whose responsibility it is to restrict cyberbullies. There are numerous online behaviors going against the law, such as stalking and harassment. Past that, few people agree whether cyberbullying is a family, school, or police issue. Only a handful of states make bullying a criminal offense, whereas the bulk of the states with bullying and cyberbullying laws simply call for school sanctions.

One dilemma facing policymakers is that most cyberbullying does not take place at school. It often takes place from home computers, tablets, and cell phones. The trend in a decade's worth of court cases shows schools have the

SEXUAL HARASSMENT CONTINUES

Despite protections against sexual discrimination under both Title IX and the Fourteenth Amendment, a 2010 survey found 48 percent of elementary teachers still report hearing sexist remarks in their schools.[4] In middle school and high school, almost half of the students surveyed reported being sexually harassed during the 2010–2011 school year.[5] Among LGBTQ students, rates of verbal sexual harassment were 85 percent and physical harassment rates were 40 percent.[6] Moreover, LGBTQ students were twice as likely to be the victims of verbal sexual harassment as their peers.[7]

right to intervene in cyberbullying events if they result in a clear disruption of the school learning environment. Nonetheless, the debate continues on how to address inappropriate use of technology within schools' current bullying policies. And, as with face-to-face bullying, policies vary widely between school districts.

The next hurdle facing cyberbullying cases is addressing the issue without infringing on First Amendment freedom of speech rights. While the US Supreme Court has not, as of 2013, tackled students'

ANTIBULLYING BILL OF RIGHTS

Following the suicide of Rutgers University freshman Tyler Clementi, New Jersey passed what is hailed as the toughest antibullying law in the nation. Effective September 1, 2011, the Antibullying Bill of Rights mandated bullying policies and procedures every public school has to follow. Details of the extensive law include staff training and student education. Schools must also create safety teams of school staff and parents. Further, schools must investigate allegations of bullying within one day of the report. Advocates believe the law's passage sends a clear message: victims will be supported and bullying will not be tolerated.

Yet not everyone is happy. Schools contend the law puts an undue burden on schools without compensation for the time and resources required to implement the Bill of Rights. Even parents are wondering if the bill is controlling everyday interactions among students. Further, some of the language defining bullying is difficult to interpret, leaving schools to determine when normal comments and jokes actually cross the line. Despite the controversy, the law is a potential model for other states to follow.

rights to free speech in the context of cyberbullying, the court maintains students do have First Amendment rights. At the same time, the court has placed limits on this. The Constitution does not protect student speech if it involves a threat; is lewd, vulgar, or profane; if the speech is school sponsored, such as through publications, performances, or other such activities; if the speech causes a disruption at school; or if the speech infringes on the rights of others.

No matter how administrators, schools, districts, and lawmakers deal with cyberbullying, they walk a fine line between their obligations to protect students and the need to avoid infringing on anyone's free speech rights. The debate is far from over and will continue to evolve alongside technology.

SOME GROUPS TAKE ISSUE AGAINST ANTIBULLYING LAWS

Some groups are opposed to antibullying legislation on the grounds of religious freedom. In areas where legislation and policy specifically mention gays and lesbians, some groups are speaking out against these policies. Evangelical groups claim that by including homosexuals in the language used by schools to prevent bullying, the schools are promoting and endorsing homosexuality and gay marriage. In Arizona, an antibullying bill was effectively killed by a Christian lobbying group because the bill encouraged LGBTQ tolerance.

CHAPTER
NINE

TAKING ACTION

Research has shown bullying is an issue in US schools and across the globe. In order to reduce or eliminate bullying, schools first need to be aware of the bullying going on and admit it is a problem. When schools take this step, it is the first toward building a better school environment. Creating a culture of caring ultimately makes school a safer place, physically, academically, and emotionally, for all students.

Prevention Programs

Olweus developed one of the earliest bullying prevention programs in 1983 in Norway. Statistical evaluations revealed the first version of the Olweus Bullying Prevention Program was highly effective. Due to its enormous success in Scandinavia, the program was adapted and implemented in US schools in the mid-1990s. Olweus's program seeks to prevent and reduce bullying at the individual, school, classroom, and community levels. In schools where this evidence-based

After Rebecca Sedwick's suicide, peers took action, calling attention to bullying and hosting a car wash fund-raiser to help Sedwick's family cover funeral costs.

87

program has been implemented, bullying is typically reduced by 30 to 50 percent.

There are currently countless other programs available to schools. The most effective programs include the whole student body, staff, and parents in education and bullying prevention. Schools also need to actively work to foster a positive and supportive school environment accepting of differences. There must also be school rules and policies related to bullying

ARE BULLYING PREVENTION PROGRAMS ALWAYS POSITIVE?

There are many antibullying programs, some of which are better than others. Experts report some programs may have unintended negative consequences. A study conducted by the University of Texas in 2013 suggests many antibullying programs actually increase incidences of physical and emotional bullying. Researchers propose some antibullying programs actually teach kids the ins and outs of bullying, giving the bully ideas about how to bully and get away with it. The University of Texas researchers suggest programs should not target certain groups. Also, zero tolerance policies punishing students for aggressive or bullying behavior often backfire because the disciplinarian is modeling rejection.

Another factor schools must consider is proper implementation. Even scientifically proven programs such as Olweus's will cause an increase in bullying if the program is not faithfully implemented. In addition, to be effective, school culture needs to change so the overall expectations and values among students and staff create a safe environment.

that are consistently enforced. Student education should define acceptable school and online behavior. Students should also know what to do if they are bullied or if they witness bullying. Other effective practices include anonymous student surveys to assess bullying issues; staff training on how to identify and respond to bullying; creating a group to coordinate bullying prevention and response efforts; and increased adult supervision in locations prone to bullying.

UNITY DAY

The wave of orange seen across the United States on Wednesday, October 9, 2013, was not in support of any sports team. Instead, PACER's National Bullying Prevention Center called on people to wear orange on that date as a way to show unity for students who have been bullied and want to see bullying end. In addition to wearing orange, the day of unity included donning orange snap bracelets and writing the word *unity* on hands and notebooks. A Facebook event was also created.

Cyberbullying

While online bullying shares many similarities with traditional bullying, cyberbullying prevention comes with a unique set of challenges. First, because cyberbullying does not involve face-to-face interaction, students are removed from seeing the immediate impact of their words or actions. Those using computers, cell

If you are the victim of or witness cyberbullying,
contact an adult who can help put a stop to it.

phones, and other forms of technology need to be taught to think before they click.

Students should also be aware of their role in cyberbullying and know what they can do to stop it. Those who witness bullying through technology need to record what they see and tell adults about what is happening. They need to learn how to avoid being a cyberbully, even accidentally. Forwarding hurtful messages or images or joining in harassing someone online make students bullies themselves.

The anonymity allowed by cyberbullying is one of the greatest challenges facing prevention. Not only does it allow the bully to remain anonymous, but it also often makes tracking and punishing cyberbullies difficult. This is why documenting and reporting to an adult are so important.

Cyberbullying needs to be specifically addressed in school bullying policies.

IT GETS BETTER PROJECT

LGBTQ youth are disproportionately targets for bullies. In an effort to support LGBTQ youth who are enduring bullying, columnist Dan Savage and his partner created a video in September 2010 to instill hope that things will get better. Since then, the It Gets Better Project has inspired tens of thousands of user-made videos from around the world. ItGetsBetter.org is a place where LGBTQ youth can witness love through support and the sharing of stories.

These policies must be clear about the extent to which schools can intervene and impose discipline in cases when off-campus cyberbullying causes a significant disruption to the school's learning environment.

Just as schools and towns are communities, so is the Internet. Everyone must take a role in creating a positive community online.

Individual Roles

It is important for those who are bullied to understand the bullying is not their fault. Since bullies look for a reaction from their target, bullied students can control the interaction by not reacting to a bully, however difficult that may be. In addition, anyone who is a victim of bullying should tell a trusted adult. Staying silent only maintains a bully's power. Bullies also seek out others who are alone, so targets should find friends to hang out with or stay near an adult.

Parents also play a critical role in preventing bullying. Open communication is key, so children should be willing to talk when bullying issues arise. Parents should also model proper interactions, communication, confidence, self-control, and empathy. All children need to be taught bullying is not okay and will not be

If you are the victim of bullying, note where the attack occurred, who was present, and report details to an adult.

tolerated. Schools and parents should help bullies learn other, more effective ways to interact with peers and deal with their emotions. Bullies should also be aware of the negative effects of their actions.

Parents can help teach children proper online etiquette and closely monitor online activity. Parents should likewise spend time with children discussing ways to deal with conflict, both online and in person. Finally, parents must communicate that inappropriate cyber behaviors will not be allowed.

In the bullying triad, the bystander wields power when it comes to putting an end to bullying. The American Psychiatric Association reviewed effective antibullying campaigns. One of the key findings calls for empowering bystanders to help victims, stand up to bullies, and report bullying behavior. Further, bystanders must understand the role they play in any bullying situation, as outlined by Olweus's bully circle. Standing silently, joining in, laughing at inappropriate jokes, and forwarding hurtful messages online are all actions that reinforce a bully's behavior. Some experts believe if schools work to empower bystanders, the kids themselves will ultimately create new norms. They are the ones who can call each other out on bullying behavior. In the end, experts hope kids will create an environment in which bullying is not acceptable, but calling it out is.

THE BULLY PROJECT

Following the production of the documentary *Bully* in 2011, filmmaker Lee Hirsch was inspired to start a national movement to end bullying. The BULLY Project began as a campaign to bring the film to 1 million students. Along with the screening, the project also provides resources, curriculum, and training focused on empathy and taking action against bullying. After reaching their goal for 1 million kids, the BULLY Project set a new goal of 10 million kids.

TIMELINE

1972
Title IX, part of the 1972 Education Amendment, is passed, prohibiting sex discrimination in any educational facility receiving federal funds. It is later invoked to protect gay, lesbian, and bisexual students from discrimination.

1973
Dan Olweus, a researcher and professor at the University of Bergen in Norway, publishes a study of bullies and their victims.

1983
Olweus implements the first version of the Olweus Bullying Prevention Program in Norway.

1996
In July, a federal court explains the constitutional responsibility of schools to protect gay students from antigay abuse in the case brought by gay teen Jamie Nabozny.

1998

Beussink v. Woodland R-IV School District is heard before a federal court after a student is punished by his school for an insulting website he had created about school officials. The court holds the boy's First Amendment rights had been violated when the school punished him, based on the fact the website did not create a disturbance at school nor did it violate anyone's civil rights.

1999

On May 24, in the case of LaShonda Davis, the Supreme Court holds schools are responsible for protecting students from sexual harassment as defined by Title IX; the shootings and deaths at Columbine High School in Colorado on April 20 prompt a tidal wave of antibullying research, legislation, policies, and programs.

1999–2010

States across the country enact more than 120 new bills to introduce or amend statutes related to bullying, including defining bullying and related behaviors more clearly in schools and establishing policies prohibiting such behavior.

2000

The term *cyberbullying* is used for the first time.

TIMELINE

2001

Neil Marr and Tim Field coin the term *bullycide* in their book *Bullycide: Death at Playtime.*

2010

On January 14, 15-year-old Phoebe Prince commits suicide after months of verbal and online bullying.

2010

The Dignity for Every Student bill, focusing on bullying prevention and education, unanimously passes in Massachusetts in May.

2010

On September 22, Rutgers University freshman Tyler Clementi commits suicide after he is secretly videotaped on a date with another man, and others in the dorm and around the world watch the live feed.

2011

In May, five teens plead guilty to criminal harassment for the bullying of Phoebe Prince.

2011

Facebook launches the Stop Bullying: Speak Up campaign in fall, urging kids, parents, and teachers to take a pledge to stand up to bullying.

2011

On September 1, New Jersey passes the Antibullying Bill of Rights, the toughest in the nation at the time.

2013

Rebecca Ann Sedwick ends her own life in September after enduring months of cyberbullying. Two classmates are charged with stalking, although the charges are eventually dropped.

2013

In October, offensive lineman Jonathan Martin walks off the Miami Dolphins team after months of bullying by teammate Richie Incognito.

ESSENTIAL FACTS

At Issue
Students are bullied in US schools every day. In one year, more than 13 million children will be the victims of bullying, with the abuse occurring at school, on the bus, in town, and in cyberspace.

Critical Dates
1972
Title IX, part of the 1972 Education Amendment, passed in the United States. Title IX prohibited sex discrimination in any educational facility receiving federal funds. It later also protected gay, lesbian, and bisexual students from discrimination.

1973
Dan Olweus, a researcher and professor at the University of Bergen in Norway, published the first large-scale scientific study of bullies and their victims. His work revealed to the public the seriousness of the bullying issue.

1983
Olweus developed one of the earliest bullying prevention programs in Norway.

mid-1990s
Olweus's bullying program was brought to the United States.

1999

The first antibullying legislation was passed in Georgia. In May, after the case of LaShonda Davis, the Supreme Court states schools are responsible for protecting students from sexual harassment.

1999–2010

More than 120 new bills to introduce or amend statutes related to bullying are enacted across the country.

2011

On September 1, New Jersey passed the Antibullying Bill of Rights.

Quote

"The label 'bullying' is really incendiary. It ratchets everything up emotionally. It makes it hard to really address, rationally, what the best course of action is." —*Elizabeth Englander, social psychologist*

GLOSSARY

attention deficit hyperactivity disorder (ADHD)
A syndrome characterized by difficulty controlling behavior, extreme activity levels, and the inability to concentrate for extended periods of time.

bystander
Someone who witnesses bullying.

cyberstalking
Repeated harassment that takes place online and includes threats of harm or that is highly intimidating and intrusive upon one's personal privacy.

depression
A mental disorder marked by sadness, inactivity, loss of interest in usual activities, feelings of dejection and hopelessness, and some physical symptoms.

hazing
The practice of forcing someone to take part in embarrassing or dangerous activities, often as a sort of initial rite.

homophobia

An irrational fear, hatred toward, or discrimination against a homosexual or homosexuality.

intervention

When one or more people become involved in a situation to influence an outcome.

perpetrator

One who engages in bully behavior.

retaliate

To get revenge on someone who has hurt you or treated you badly.

victimization

The act of purposely discriminating against someone.

ADDITIONAL RESOURCES

Selected Bibliography

Bazelon, Emily. *Sticks and Stones.* New York: Random, 2013. Print.

Coloroso, Barbara. *The Bully, the Bullied and the Bystander.* New York: Collins Living, 2008. Print.

Kowalski, Robin M., Susan P. Limber, and Patricia W. Agatston. *Cyber Bullying.* Malden, MA: Blackwell, 2008. Print.

Kuykendall, Sally. *Bullying: Health & Medical Issues Today.* Denver, CO: Greenwood, 2012. Print.

Olweus, Dan. *Bullying at School: What We Know and What We Can Do.* Oxford, UK: Blackwell, 1993. Print.

Further Readings

Ludwig, Trudy. *Confessions of a Former Bully.* Berkeley: Tricycle, 2010. Print.

Palacio, R. J. *Wonder.* New York: Knopf, 2012. Print.

Simmons, Rachel. *Odd Girl Out, Revised and Updated: The Hidden Culture of Aggression in Girls.* Boston: Houghton, 2011. Print.

Websites

To learn more about Essential Issues, visit **booklinks.abdopublishing.com**. These links are routinely monitored and updated to provide the most current information available.

For More Information

For more information on this subject, contact or visit the following organizations:

PACER Center, Inc
8161 Normandale Blvd.
Bloomington, MN 55437
888-248-0822
http://www.pacerteensagainstbullying.org
PACER provides tools for identifying and responding to bullying.

Safe2Tell
PO Box 49296
Colorado Springs, CO 80949
719-520-7435
http://safe2tell.org
Safe2Tell offers a confidential means to report any bullying or threatening behaviors.

SOURCE NOTES

Chapter 1. The New Girl

1. Kevin Cullen. "The Untouchable Mean Girls." *Boston.com*. Boston Globe, 24 Jan. 2010. Web. 1 Nov. 2013.

2. Erik Eckholm and Katie Zezima. "6 Teenagers Are Charged After Classmate's Suicide." *New York Times*. New York Times, 29 Mar. 2010. Web. 1 Nov. 2013.

3. Ibid.

4. "Nationwide Bullying Statistics." *Sears*. Sears Brands, LLC, n.d. Web. 1 Nov. 2013.

5. Catharine M. Young. "Teen Bullying & Suicide: What You Should Know." *Senator Catharine M. Young*. NYSenate.gov, Feb. 2013. Web. 1 Nov. 2013.

6. Ibid.

Chapter 2. What Is Bullying?

1. Dan Olweus. "Dr. Olweus on Bullying." *Olweus Bullying Prevention Program*. Olweus Bullying Prevention Program, n.d. Web. 11 Nov. 2013.

2. "Bullying." *American Psychological Association*. American Psychological Association, n.d. Web. 16 Nov. 2013.

3. Joseph G. Kosciw, et al. "The 2009 National School Climate Survey." *GLSEN*. Gay, Lesbian and Straight Education Network, 2010. Web. 16 Dec. 2013.

4. "It's a Girl's World." *YouTube*. YouTube, 7 Nov. 2012. Web. 11 Nov. 2013.

5. Ibid.

Chapter 3. Cyberbullying

1. Justin W. Patchin. "2010." *Cyberbullying Research Center*. Cyberbullying Research Center, 9 July 2013. Web. 2 Nov. 2013.

2. Justin W. Patchin. "Summary of Our Research (2004–2013)." *Cyberbullying Research Center*. Cyberbullying Research Center, 10 July 2013. Web. 2 Nov. 2013.

3. Amy Harmon. "Internet Gives Teenage Bullies Weapons to Wound From Afar." *New York Times*. New York Times, 26 Aug. 2004. Web. 2 Nov. 2013.

4. "Cyber Support Me." *PBS-Finding Scotland's Real Heroes*. STV Player, 20 Sept. 2013. Web. 6 Nov. 2013.

5. Tamara Lush. "Cyberbullying Charges Weighed after Suicide of Florida Girl, 12." *Washington Post*. Washington Post, 13 Sept. 2013. Web. 2 Nov. 2013.

6. Sameer Hinduja. "Cyberbullying Fact Sheet: Identification, Prevention and Response." *Cyberbullying Research Center*. Cyberbullying Research Center, 30 Dec. 2010. Web. 1 Nov. 2013.

Chapter 4. The Bully

1. "Are We Too Quick to Call 'Bully'?" *ABC15.com: Taking Action*. Scripps TV Station Group, 4 Oct. 2013. Web. 8 Nov. 2013.

2. Pamela Paul. "The Playground Gets Even Tougher." *New York Times*. New York Times, 8 Oct. 2010. Web. 4 Nov. 2013.

Chapter 5. The Bullied

1. "Youth Risk Behavior Surveillance—United States 2011." *MMWR*. Centers for Disease Control and Prevention, 8 June 2012. Web. 8 Nov. 2013.

2. Ibid.

3. Ibid.

4. "Gay Bullying." *National Youth Association*. National Youth Association, 7 Nov. 2010. Web. 8 Nov. 2013.

5. Maria L. La Ganga. "A Grieving Father Touches a Life." *Los Angeles Times*. Los Angeles Times, 14 Oct. 2013. Web. 8 Nov. 2013.

6. *Joe's Walk for Change*. Joe's Walk for Change, 2013. Web. 8 Nov. 2013.

7. Barbara Coloroso. *The Bully, the Bullied, and the Bystander*. New York: Collins Living, 2008. Print. 48.

8. "Bullying of Brothers and Sisters Should Not Be Ignored." *American Academy of Pediatrics*. American Academy of Pediatrics, 17 June 2013. Web. 8 Nov. 2013.

Chapter 6. The Bystander

1. "What Is the Bystander Effect?" *Psychology Today*. Sussex Publishers, LLC, n.d. Web. 8 Nov. 2013.

2. "Playground Bullies: Canada Combats a Deadly Threat." *Ethics Newsline*. Institute for Global Ethics, 1 Apr. 2002. Web. 10 Nov. 2013.

3. "Statistics." *The Family Resource Facilitation Program*. The Family Resource Facilitation Program, n.d. Web. 16 Dec. 2013.

SOURCE NOTES CONTINUED

Chapter 7. The Effects of Bullying

1. "Welcome." *Alliance School*. Milwaukee Public Schools, n.d. Web. 16 Dec. 2013.

2. David Carroll. "Tyler Long's Family Responds to Murray Schools Request for Funds." *WRCB TV – Chattanooga*. WorldNow and WRCB, 19 July 2013. Web. 11 Nov. 2013.

3. "Facts About Bullying." *Bullying Prevention Program*. Bully Free Systems, n.d. Web. 1 Nov. 2013.

4. Ibid.

5. Ibid.

6. Jessie Klein. *The Bully Society*. New York: New York UP, 2012. Print. 1.

7. Robin M. Kowalski, et al. *Cyber Bullying*. Malden, MA: Blackwell, 2008. Print. 27.

8. "Adult Bullying." *PBS*. Vulcan Productions, n.d. Web. 2 Nov. 2013.

9. Anna Mikulak. "Far From Being Harmless, the Effects of Bullying Last Long into Adulthood." *Association for Psychological Science*. Association for Psychological Science, 19 Aug. 2013. Web. 11 Nov. 2013.

10. "Facts About Bullying." *Bullying Prevention Program*. Bully Free Systems, n.d. Web. 1 Nov. 2013.

Chapter 8. Legislation

1. "Megan Meier Cyberbullying Prevention Act." *Cyberbullying*. University of North Carolina at Chapel Hill, n.d. Web. 11 Nov. 2013.

2. "H.R. 1199: Safe Schools Improvement Act of 2013." *Govtrack.us*. Civic Impulse, LLC, 14 Mar. 2013. Web. 11 Nov. 2013.

3. "The Next Generation of Title IX: Harassment and Bullying Based on Sex." *NWLC.org*. National Women's Law Center, June 2012. Web. 11 Nov. 2013.

4. Ibid

5. Ibid.

6. Ibid.

7. Ibid.

Chapter 9. Taking Action

None.

INDEX

adult bullies, 73
Alliance School, 68
Antibullying Bill of Rights, 84
antibullying campaigns, 30, 61, 94, 95

Bell, Jadin, 52
Bell, Joe, 52
books about bullying, 17–18, 19, 40, 53, 70
BULLY Project, the, 95
bullying circle, 58–59, 65, 94
Bullying Prevention Program, 19, 75, 87–89
Bush, Elizabeth, 53
bystander effect, 58
bystanders, 11, 17, 28, 44, 57–64, 67, 68, 94

Centers for Disease Control (CDC), 15, 47
characteristics of a bully, 37–38
Clementi, Tyler, 57, 84
Columbine High School, 77
cost of bullying, 74
court cases, 11–13, 35, 59, 70, 78–82
cyberbullying, 19, 25, 27–35, 39, 41, 44, 47, 52, 61, 62, 68, 77–78, 81, 83–85, 89–92

Davis, LaShonda, 81
DearBully.com, 53
definition of bullying, 19–20

depression, 9, 15, 32, 40, 68, 73, 74
Dignity for Every Student bill, 11
disabilities, 49, 70

emotional bullying, 23, 40, 89
Englander, Elizabeth, 38

Facebook, 9, 28, 33, 52, 61, 89
Fourteenth Amendment, 78–79, 81, 83
free speech, 35, 84–85

gender, 23, 37, 40–41, 47, 82

happy slapping, 33
harassment, 8, 11, 13, 21, 23, 30–31, 32, 43, 44, 48, 59, 70, 72, 74, 77, 78, 80–83
hazing, 43
history of bullying, 17–19
homophobia, 23, 79, 85

It Gets Better Project, 91
It's a Girl's World, 25

labeling bullies, 38, 45, 74–75
laws and policies, 8, 11, 12, 15, 21, 25, 77–78, 83–84, 85, 88, 91–92
LGBTQ bullying, 11, 23, 49, 52, 67, 68, 79–80, 82, 83, 85, 91

Long, Tyler, 70–71
long-term effects
    bullies, 45, 74–75
    victims, 73–74

Marcuson, Amanda, 30
Martin, Jonathan, 48
Massachusetts Commission Against
    Discrimination, 13
media, 8, 44, 52, 61, 94
Meier, Megan, 78
movies about bullying, 18

Nabozny, Jamie, 79–80
National Football League, 48

O'Connor, Sandra Day, 81
Olweus, Dan, 18–19, 58–59, 65,
    73, 75, 87, 88, 94

parents, 11, 13, 34, 38, 41, 44, 45,
    50, 52, 61, 71, 84, 88, 92–93, 94
physical bullying, 17, 20–22,
    38–41, 55, 64, 70, 81, 89
popularity, 9, 17, 38, 39, 40, 49
prevention, 11, 15, 19, 62, 65, 70,
    75, 77, 78, 81, 85, 87–89, 91–93
Prince, Phoebe, 7–15

racism, 21
Ravi, Dharun, 57
reasons for bullying, 41–45

Safe2Tell.org, 62
Scheibel, Elizabeth, 11–12
school environment, 41, 59, 71, 75,
    81, 84, 87, 88, 92, 95
school shootings, 71, 73, 77
Sedwick, Rebecca Ann, 31, 32
self-injury, 9, 50, 64
sexual bullying, 21–23, 74, 80–82,
    83
sibling bullying, 55
South Hadley High School, 7, 11
stalking, 11, 31, 32, 39, 83
suicide, 9, 12, 15, 38, 52, 62,
    67–68, 70, 71, 84
Support Me campaign, 30

teachers, 11, 38, 52, 61–62, 83
text messages, 8, 17, 27, 28, 33, 48
Title IX, 81–82, 83

Unity Day, 89

verbal bullying, 21, 40, 59, 64, 70

Walker-Hoover, Carl Joseph, 11
warning signs, 50, 52
Wesley, Dawn-Marie, 59
Woodham, Luke, 73

ABOUT THE AUTHOR

Laura Perdew is a former middle school teacher turned author. She writes for children of all ages, including numerous titles for the education market and a guide for parents traveling through Colorado with small children, *Kids on the Move! Colorado*. She lives and plays in Boulder, Colorado, with her husband and twin boys.

ABOUT THE CONSULTANT

Sally Kuykendall is a nurse, researcher, and university professor. She is an early pioneer of bullying prevention in the United States. She lives with her husband near Philadelphia, where she enjoys time with her three sons and two stepdaughters. She continues to pursue her passion of advocating for youth and children.